THE BUCKET LIST
JOURNAL

THIS JOURNAL BELONGS TO

First published in the United States of America in 2020 by Universe Publishing,
A Division of Rizzoli International Publications, Inc.
300 Park Avenue South
New York, NY 10010
www.rizzoliusa.com

2020 2021 2022 2023 / 10 9 8 7 6 5 4 3 2 1

ISBN: 978-0-7893-3770-2
Library of Congress Control Number: 2020937086

Visit us online:
Facebook.com/RizzoliNewYork
Twitter: @Rizzoli_Books
Instagram.com/RizzoliBooks
Pinterest.com/RizzoliBooks
Youtube.com/user/RizzoliNY
Issuu.com/Rizzoli

Conceived, designed, and produced by
The Bright Press, an imprint of the Quarto Group
The Old Brewery
6 Blundell Street
London N7 9BH
United Kingdom
T 00 44 20 7700 6700
www.QuartoKnows.com

Publisher: James Evans
Editorial Director: Isheeta Mustafi
Art Director: Katherine Radcliffe
Design and Additional Art Direction: Studio Noel
Project Manager and Author: Kath Stathers
Managing Editor: Jacqui Sayers
Senior Editor: Caroline Elliker
Editorial Assistant: Chloë Porter
Picture Researcher: Jenny Quiggin

Printed and bound in China

THE BUCKET LIST
JOURNAL

WRITE YOUR OWN ADVENTURE

UNIVERSE

WELCOME TO YOUR NEXT ADVENTURE!

Use the pages of this book to plan and record your bucket list of dreams and ambitions, from once-in-a-lifetime trips to far-flung locations to short hops and fun experiences you can enjoy closer to home.

Travel offers no guarantees, and it's quite possible to turn up when your must-see museum is closed, or due to the many quirks of the natural world, your plan to see the Golden Gate Bridge could be thwarted by something as simple as a little sea fog. But with a little bit of careful planning you can avoid most upsets. Always remember a true adventurer plans to the finest detail, but then has the flexibility and spirit to enjoy the unexpected challenges that come along the way. What is life without risk? Enjoy the chaos and be sure to keep your memories forever, in the pages of this book.

Wherever you travel, help preserve what you see for future generations. Don't put yourself in harm's way seeking the perfect moment—take only memories and leave only footprints.

HOW TO USE THIS JOURNAL

Throughout the book you can find Trip Diaries and blank journaling pages to record your travels (page 30 onward). These include ruled pages for writing alongside unlined pages you can use to draw your memories or paste in photographs and memorabilia from your travels.

Planning Information
At the back of the book you can find some handy advice
and useful lists to make traveling a breeze.

HOW TO KEEP A JOURNAL

We wanderers, ever seeking the lonelier way, begin no day where we have ended another day; and no sunrise finds us where sunset left us. Even while the earth sleeps we travel. We are the seeds of the tenacious plant, and it is in our ripeness and our fullness of heart that we are given to the wind and are scattered.

From *The Prophet* by Kahlil Gibran

Living an adventure, writing about it, and reflecting back upon it can bring a good deal of pleasure. It can help us learn more about ourselves and our expectations—as well as providing us with vivid recollections that might otherwise be lost to the mists of time.

A travel journal isn't necessarily an itinerary of where you went and what you saw. You can add your anticipation of events, your motivation for going to places, what you imagined things would be like, as well as what the reality was. And that reality goes beyond the sights; it's the sounds, the smells, the people, the weather, the things you thought about, and the decisions you made from day to day—all the different elements that go into creating memories.

Many people who start keeping a journal find that they are able to unlock creative and meditative aspects of their personality. You can use the pages of a journal to help deal with the joy, and the sorrow, that moving from one place to another can bring.

Just as every journey begins with a single step, a journal begins with just a few words. If you are unsure how to begin, write a small dedication to yourself at the beginning of this book (page 1). What do you want this journal—and journey—to do?

FIVE GOLDEN RULES

1

Where and when

Note the date and where you are when you write. When you are journeying from place to place and may even be short of a little sleep, those little details get lost alarmingly fast. For the same reason, try to write in the moment. If you save writing for the evenings, you will be recalling an experience, and worse, you may fall asleep before you start!

2

Include other people

The people you meet are a huge part of the traveling experience. Whether it's fellow travelers or locals, you can learn from others, and a journal is the perfect place to record it all. Write down local sayings and funny things you hear, as well as all the in-jokes that develop along the way.

3

Look forward as well as back

Use your journal to think about and plan where you're going and what you want to do there. Comparing your expectations to the reality makes for very interesting reading. Plus when you meet people coming the other way, you can make a note of any tips they give you for future destinations.

4

Focus on the detail

While you'll see some amazing sights on your journeys, sometimes it can be the mundane events that will make you smile years down the line.

5

Be honest and keep it real

Traveling can change us. We put ourselves outside our comfort zones and learn things about the world and about ourselves. Not every experience we have is a delight, and it's normal to miss things about home, even while you are having the time of your life. Use your journal to reflect on all parts of a trip, the good and the bad, to help you get a grip on all the different feelings you have. And if you are having a bad day? Turn back a few pages and remember something fun.

LIFE IS EITHER A DARING ADVENTURE OR NOTHING AT ALL.

HELEN KELLER

Begin your journey by reflecting back on some of your proudest moments.
What makes you feel courageous?

100 EXPERIENCES FOR YOUR
BUCKET LIST

Use this list of amazing activities to plot your own adventures.

▶ 1. Watch whales breach
Witness these giants of the deep surface for a few precious moments.

2. Sail to a small island
The sun sparkling on the water and wind billowing in the sails—it seems like sailing is how nature wanted us to travel.

3. Follow the wildebeest migration
Although any large-scale migration is exhilarating, the thunder of hooves as thousands of wildebeest follow the rains in Africa is something special.

4. Bag a Munro (or a mountaintop)
There are 282 Munros—mountains over 3,000 ft (914.4 m)—in Scotland alone. How many peaks can you climb?

5. Go to the ballet
Be astounded by the grace and superhuman abilities of pro dancers.

6. See six million birds or more
Murmurations of starlings and other flocks of birds performing their massive aerobatics can be seen from Somerset, England, to Israel's Negev desert, and many other places in between.

7. Swim in the seven seas
It's a challenge that will make you travel to places you've not heard of yet.

8. Learn to play the ukulele
Or the marimba. You are sure to boost your musical skills in the land of an instrument's birth.

9. See a scene and go there
Take a spontaneous trip to somewhere new, inspired by nothing more than a photograph or painting.

10. Get on your bike
Pedal right across the flat landscape of a foreign country or look out for places like canal routes that are perfect for beginners.

11. See a field of flowers
From tulips to peony or lavender farms, feed your senses in these perfumed, rainbow-striped fields.

12. Remember the past
Visit a monument or historical place that connects you to humanity.

13. Travel for art
Pick a painting you have always wanted to see in person (check it's on view before you travel).

14. Float in the Dead Sea
Enjoy weightlessness in the world's lowest sea.

15. Learn to climb
Whether you do it for the view or the achievement factor, they're both worth it!

16. Visit the home of a literary hero
Connect with a maestro as you see where they wrote their works of art.

17. Ride in a classic automobile
Appreciate the days when cars were more about style and less about speed.

18. Feel the wind beneath your wings
Paraglide off the side of a hill for a sense of calm—mixed with extreme adrenaline.

19. Hear a glacier move
Contemplate the passage of time and the beauty of nature as you listen to the creaks of a glacier.

20. Hear the howling of wolves
Listen out for the call of the wild with the unmistakable sound of wolves in their native land.

21. Jump into a freezing lake
Brace yourself and jump. Feel the exhilaration of being submerged in ice-cold water.

22. Take a road trip
Slow down the pace, put on some tunes, and watch the scenery drift on by.

23. Become a work of art
Here's one idea: Join a Spencer Tunick event! Take off your clothes and pose in a crowd of nudes for an artwork you'll never forget.

24. Watch penguins waddle
To see these creatures in their natural habitat is an uplifting adventure—you can't help but smile when you're in the company of penguins.

25. Trek a long-distance path from start to finish
Feel the accomplishment of a long hike, with the added bonus of spectacular natural views.

26. See a desert bloom
In places like the Atacama Desert when the rains arrive, where there should be sand, suddenly there are endless flowers.

▼ 27. Swim in a sea of natural phosphorescence
Paint with your limbs in a sea aglow with plankton.

28. Travel an epic overland route

Pick any form of transport you like and follow the silk road through Charyn Canyon, Kazakhstan.

29. Learn a foreign language

Add an extra dimension to the places you travel to and learn from the locals (start on page 188 of this book).

30. Scale a volcano

Feel the connection to Earth's most powerful forces from the top of a volcano.

31. Bake a loaf of local bread

Learn one of the most traditional skills of them all—with a gourmet guide.

32. Experience an eclipse

Come alive as the world goes dark in this most emotional of natural phenomena.

33. Eat in a world-rated restaurant

From Michelin stars to up-and-coming celebrities of the culinary world, treat yourself to the best of the best, even just for one night only.

34. Swim somewhere wild

Submerge yourself in the freshness of an outdoor pool. Pool or river—always check it's safe before you swim.

35. Rock out at a summer festival

Glastonbury's atmosphere is legendary—or maybe Coachella is on your list?

36. Ride on a steam train

All aboard! The most romantic way to travel.

37. Walk on a rope bridge

In Taman Negara National Park in Malaysia you can walk through the tree canopy on a rope bridge that's one-third of a mile long.

▶ 38. Cruise along an ancient river

You'll float through one of the world's most impressive gorges if you can visit the Yangtze River in China.

39. Measure up to a giraffe

Visit a natural park and see this tallest of all creatures.

40. Let architecture blow your mind

From the world's tallest building to the oldest.

41. Skip a stone

If you are really good at this, why not join the world championship? The competition is held annually on Easdale Island in Scotland.

42. Hike in the Himalayas

The scenery is stunning, and you can see Mount Everest!

43. Watch bears climb a tree

Marvel at how something so large and fierce can be so nimble.

44. Go exotic bird-watching

Perhaps you'll see a toucan—could you fit more color on one bird's bill?

45. Spend a night in a tent

Slow down and live in a yurt for a while.

46. Lie on a beach in the Caribbean

Enjoy miles of white sand and palm trees.

47. Climb a tall tower

For something a bit different, go to Gaudí's Sagrada Família in Barcelona, Spain—a wild and inspiring cathedral where work began on March 19, 1882, and it's still not finished!

48. Sleep under the northern lights

In some locations you can sleep in a transparent "bubble" tent as northern lights paint the sky.

◀ 49. Or sleep up in a tree

Tree houses aren't just for kids, and they are often great eco-friendly adventures.

50. Swim naked

Feel a connection to nature with a skinny dip.

51. Eat pizza in old Napoli

Some things just taste better in their original home.

52. Visit Norway's fjords

So beautiful, with an accessible hiking route too.

53. See piranhas . . . from a safe distance!

Keep your toes out of the water as you hunt for these toothy aquatic beasts.

54. Drink tequila in Tequila, Mexico

Call it educational and tour a distillery to see how the drink is made.

55. Trek on every continent

From snow to desert, mountains to valleys, create a path to remember.

56. Watch sea otters chilling

In places like Moss Landing in California you can see these wonderful animals lying on their backs as they munch on fish.

57. Dive to a wreck

Travel back in time as you explore a past life on the ocean's floor.

58. Marvel at a temple

Be inspired by the faith of others.

59. Help protect an endangered species

Volunteer at a registered conservation project (be alert to fake conservation projects).

60. Walk behind a waterfall

See the world from a different angle.

61. Rappel down a rock face

Trust yourself to the ropes as you leap backward into the void.

62. Learn a traditional dance

It takes two to tango, but only if you know the steps.

63. Travel in style

Cross a country or a whole continent in style, on a train where fine dining and luxury lounges come as standard.

64. Paddle around an iceberg

What better way to see an iceberg than from atop a stand-up paddleboard?

65. Sleep under the stars

You can see thousands of twinkling balls of gas in the night skies above unpopulated areas. Go on, count them!

66. Blow kisses to the fishes

Dive in the Red Sea and you may just meet one of the world's most friendly reef fish, a Napoleon wrasse.

67. Hear an owl hoot in the dark

Feel like you're in a children's story when you hear an owl's distinctive tu-whit, tu-whoo.

68. Race on a zip line

Find a giant double zip line so you can race a friend. (Try the Alps's La Bee—Val Thorens' double zip line.)

69. Forage for food

Dig into your inner hunter-gatherer as you find your food in nature—but ensure you check with an expert before eating anything you find.

70. Find castles and pretty houses
Smile and enjoy the fact that not all houses need to have corners.

71. Visit a fabulous spa
Enjoy an ancient therapy treatment.

72. Do the Olympic bobsled run
Not for the fainthearted, in places like La Plagne, France, you'll find one heck of a riiiiiiide.

73. Or scare yourself silly on a roller-coaster
Seek out the world's longest roller-coaster ride.

74. Cut a perfect line in powder snow
Ski or snowboard: Challenge yourself to cut one continuous line through virgin snow.

75. Visit Venice
There's nowhere quite like it; the streets are made of water.

76. Trace your origins
Find out where you came from, then visit the land of your ancestors.

77. Marvel at the Romans
Seek out a Roman viaduct.

78. Drive on a racetrack
Test your nerve on the Nürburgring in Germany.

79. Be awed by the Grand Canyon
Some natural wonders really do have to be seen to be believed.

◀ 80. Drive on one of the world's finest roads

Indulge your inner car geek as you glide around a myriad hairpin bends, or embrace the rocky roads of Valley of Fire State Park, Nevada.

81. Eat pad thai in Thailand

Tickle your taste buds with some of the best street food in the world.

82. Stay in a penthouse suite

Enjoy a taste of luxury someplace absolutely fabulous and worth the splurge.

83. Run a marathon

Set yourself a challenge that has a rewarding finish.

84. Drink a fresh coconut

Sit on a beach and sip nature's health-giving elixir, fresh from the tree.

85. Stay up all night

Find an amazing spot from which to watch the sun go down—and come up.

86. Sleep in a hammock

Swing yourself to sleep in a tropical paradise.

87. See a peacock fan its feathers

The preening dandy of nature is truly inspiring. Karnataka in India has two peacock sanctuaries you can visit.

88. Go to the top of the Empire State Building

It's an icon for a reason.

89. Follow the sardine run

See the seas bubble as thousands of sardines migrate—followed by their predators.

90. Wander in a Seuss-inspired landscape

In places like Hitachi Seaside Park in Japan, you can find endless, hilarious tufts of pink Kochia.

91. Party under a full moon

Search for the perfect moonlit party spot.

92. Ride a hot-air balloon over fairy towers

If you are planning a hot-air balloon ride, why not sail over Cappadocia, Turkey, to see clusters of fairy chimneys?

93. Bet it all on black

Channel your inner James Bond and play fast and loose in one of the world's best casino towns.

94. Learn about ancient civilizations

Visit a city of ruins and discover how similar we are to our forebears.

95. Indulge in alternative pampering

Be buried in hot sand or let fish nibble on your toes—if nothing else, it makes for a good story.

96. Ride a stage of the Tour de France

Join 15,000 other cyclists in one of the world's best mass cycling events.

97. Walk in a jungle

Feel watched without knowing quite why.

98. Stumble upon an oasis

These beautiful, cooling spots look and feel like a miracle you'll be so glad to see.

99. Get lost in a maze

Rediscover your inner child as you navigate a labyrinth of green. Try the Villa Pisani Labyrinth in Stra, Italy.

100. Sing karaoke in a booth

Indulge in one of Japan's favorite pastimes—belt your heart out!

MY BUCKET LIST

Create your own personal bucket list with where you want
to go and what you want do while you're there.

PLACES TO GO AND THINGS TO DO ✓

1

2

3

4

5

6

7

8

9

10

11

12

13

14

15

16

17

18

19

20

21

22

23

24

25

26

27

28

29

30

31

32

33

34

35

36

37

38

39

40

41

42

43

44

45

46

47

48

49

50

A JOURNEY
OF A THOUSAND
MILES BEGINS WITH
A SINGLE STEP.

LAOZI

What wonderful adventures can you have close to home? List some
of the things you have been meaning to try in your local area.

—1—
TRIP DIARY

WHERE   DATE

....

STANDOUT EXPERIENCE

....

....

....

THE MOMENT I'LL ALWAYS REMEMBER

....

....

....

SOMETHING NEW I LEARNED

....

PEOPLE I MET

....

FOOD I ATE

....

MUSIC I LISTENED TO

....

....

──2──

TRIP DIARY

WHERE   DATE

....

STANDOUT EXPERIENCE

....

....

....

THE MOMENT I'LL ALWAYS REMEMBER

....

....

....

SOMETHING NEW I LEARNED

....

PEOPLE I MET

....

FOOD I ATE

....

MUSIC I LISTENED TO

....

....

TOP 20
NATURAL WONDERS OF THE WORLD

Be awed by these twenty must-see wonders created by nature.

1. Northern lights
Sámiland, Finland

Is anything more awe-inspiring than the sky being painted in streaks of green?

▼ 2. Firefall
Yosemite National Park, California

For a few days each year the setting sun lights up Horsetail Fall, making it glow like lava—a stunning spectacle known as the firefall.

3. Amazon River
Manaus, Brazil

Snaking through the rain forest, the Amazon is a powerhouse of nature.

4. Uluṟu
Northern Territory, Australia

Sacred and stunning—be sure to stay for sunset.

5. Salar de Uyuni
Uyuni, Bolivia
This huge expanse of white salt flats is one of the trippiest landscapes out there.

6. Milford Sound
South Island, New Zealand
So much beauty and peace along one stretch of water, it's sublime.

7. Hạ Long Bay
Northeast Vietnam
Emerald waters and towering limestone rocks with lush forest cascading down their sides make this a wonderful spot.

8. The Grand Canyon
Arizona
The layers and layers of colored strata and its vast expanse explain why this canyon really is the grandest of them all.

9. Iguazu Falls
Brazil/Argentina border
Feel the spray of these thundering horseshoe-shaped falls that make you glad to be alive.

10. The Matterhorn
Zermatt, Switzerland
Its steep sides and near symmetrical form make this an epic mountain peak.

11. Ngorongoro Crater
Northern Tanzania
Quite apart from the abundance of wildlife, to see the rim of a volcano this large, from the inside, is mind-blowing.

12. Verdon Gorge
Castellane, France
Start at the top of the 2,300 ft (700 m) high ravine, marveling at the turquoise waters below, then end by kayaking on the river. Heaven.

13. Mount Fuji
Honshu, Japan
If you have to choose one symmetrical, snow-capped volcano, choose this one.

14. Giant's Causeway
County Antrim, Northern Ireland
Interlocking basalt columns so neat, it's a wonder they are naturally formed.

15. Moraine Lake
Banff National Park, Canada
In a country full of superlative beauty, this lake is the epitome.

16. Table Mountain
Cape Town, South Africa
Marvel at the table-top flatness of this iconic rock.

17. Grand Prismatic Spring
Yellowstone National Park, Wyoming
Not just the country's largest hot spring, but its most epically colored too.

18. White Sands National Park
New Mexico
These dunes made of gypsum are so white you've got to wear shades.

19. Great Barrier Reef
East coast of Australia
The corals, the fish, the islands, the beaches—the reef forms them all.

20. Avenue of the Baobabs
Menabe, Madagascar
Marvel at these majestic, water-storing trees lined up like sentinels along the road.

—3—

TRIP DIARY

WHERE   DATE

....

STANDOUT EXPERIENCE

....

....

....

THE MOMENT I'LL ALWAYS REMEMBER

....

....

....

SOMETHING NEW I LEARNED

....

PEOPLE I MET

....

FOOD I ATE

....

MUSIC I LISTENED TO

....

....

ONE DOESN'T DISCOVER NEW LANDS WITHOUT CONSENTING TO LOSE SIGHT OF THE SHORE FOR A VERY LONG TIME.

ANDRÉ GIDE

What new experiences do you want to try to get you out of your comfort zone?

—4—

TRIP DIARY

WHERE   DATE

....

STANDOUT EXPERIENCE

....

....

....

THE MOMENT I'LL ALWAYS REMEMBER

....

....

....

SOMETHING NEW I LEARNED

....

PEOPLE I MET

....

FOOD I ATE

....

MUSIC I LISTENED TO

....

....

TOP 20
MAN-MADE WONDERS

Stretching back through the ages, these are humankind's greatest monuments.

1. Great Wall of China
Northern China

With over 3,000 mi (4,800 km) of wall, this is the longest structure ever made—now that's a wonder worth traveling for.

2. Tikal
Northern Guatemala

Watch the sun rise from the top of a pyramid in a lost Mayan city.

3. Angkor Wat
Siem Reap, Cambodia

Lose yourself in Buddhism in the world's largest religious monument.

4. Taj Mahal
Uttar Pradesh, India

Marvel at the power of love at the world's most romantic tomb.

5. Bagan temples
Myanmar

Seen from above, the beauty of Bagan's temples rising from the forest is hard to beat.

6. Moai
Rapa Nui, Chile

Feel the gaze of more than 800 towering stone heads on Easter Island.

7. Colosseum
Rome, Italy

Those Romans knew a thing or two about stadium building.

8. Christ the Redeemer
Rio de Janeiro, Brazil

Probably the world's most stylish landmark.

9. The Pyramids of Giza
Giza, Egypt

A feat of engineering and an archaeologist's dream.

10. Eiffel Tower
Paris, France

Will you take the elevator or the 1,710 steps to the top of France's most famous icon?

▶ 11. Machu Picchu
Cuzco, Peru

Marvel at the 500-year-old Inca buildings, still standing without any mortar.

12. Stonehenge
Wiltshire, United Kingdom

Ponder on the mystery of where the mystical stones came from.

13. La Sagrada Família
Barcelona, Spain

Bask in the quirkiness of Antoni Gaudí's unfinished masterpiece of a cathedral.

14. Chichen Itza
Yucatán, Mexico

Be amazed by the magnificent Mayan metropolis.

15. Sigiriya
Central Province, Sri Lanka

Admire the king who built his palace on a rock.

16. Parthenon
Athens, Greece
Five hundred years before Christ, the ancient Greeks built this magnificent temple dedicated to Athena.

17. Supertree Grove
Gardens by the Bay, Singapore
Modern-day spectacles that create a visual—and useful—attraction.

18. Statue of Liberty
New York City
Say hello to the lady who has welcomed generations of immigrants to the United States.

19. Millau Viaduct
Millau, France
Cross this elegant viaduct that seems to enhance the landscape below.

20. Sheikh Zayed Grand Mosque
Abu Dhabi, United Arab Emirates
Be awed by the eighty-two domes and wide expanses of white marble in this elegant building.

—5—

TRIP DIARY

WHERE   DATE

....

STANDOUT EXPERIENCE

....

....

....

THE MOMENT I'LL ALWAYS REMEMBER

....

....

....

SOMETHING NEW I LEARNED

....

PEOPLE I MET

....

FOOD I ATE

....

MUSIC I LISTENED TO

....

....

TOP 12
FOODIE DESTINATIONS

Here are twelve fabulous destinations you may not have thought of, and some amazing dishes to try.

1. Donostia-San Sebastián, Spain

What to eat: Pintxos

Every bar is foodie heaven with beautifully presented, bite-size treats lining the countertops.

2. Osaka, Japan

What to eat: Takoyaki, okonomiyaki, and ikayaki

Known as the nation's pantry, Osaka has an abundance of fresh ingredients and some of the most popular dishes in Japan.

3. Lima, Peru

What to eat: Ceviche

Peru's capital city is a rising star in the international food scene, with tantalizing options for foodies of all budgets.

4. Addis Ababa, Ethiopia

What to eat: Injera

Injera isn't just what you eat, but how you eat in Ethiopia—tearing off strips of spongy pancake to scoop up the mouthwatering spicy stews of lentils, beans, vegetables, and meat that top it.

5. Seoul, South Korea

What to eat: Chimaek

Put chicken with *maekju* (Korean for beer) and you have chimaek—succulent and crispy double-fried chicken washed down with ice-cold beer.

6. Beirut, Lebanon

What to eat: Falafel

Beirut has a burgeoning food scene, but don't leave without trying its world-beating falafel.

7. Zanzibar, Tanzania

What to eat: Anything at the Night Market in Stone Town

Every evening, chefs fill Forodhani Gardens, grilling meat and seafood, cooking soup, and frying donuts. Just look for the lines with the most locals to get the best food.

8. Mysore, India

What to eat: Dosa

Famed for its vegetarian cuisine, eat a different style of dosa every day in this southern Indian city.

9. Malmö, Sweden

What to eat: Anything foraged

A hub of hipster foodie heaven with a strong focus on superlative coffee and locally foraged ingredients.

10. Sydney, Australia

What to eat: Freshly caught and cooked seafood at the Sydney Fish Market

Soak up the vibrant colors, sights, and smells of this bustling portside market, before indulging in some fresh-cooked fish at one of its many food stalls.

11. Marrakesh, Morocco

What to eat: Ask for fresh saffron

Rahba Kedima, also known as Spice Square, is a beautiful treat for the senses, abounding with bright colors and towering pots of exuberant spices.

▶ 12. Paris, France

What to eat: Bread and cheese

Many people travel to Paris without enjoying a local market. Try Marche d'Aligre on weekday mornings.

6

TRIP DIARY

WHERE   DATE

....

STANDOUT EXPERIENCE

....

....

....

THE MOMENT I'LL ALWAYS REMEMBER

....

....

....

SOMETHING NEW I LEARNED

....

PEOPLE I MET

....

FOOD I ATE

....

MUSIC I LISTENED TO

....

....

I TRAVEL NOT
TO GO ANYWHERE,
BUT TO GO.

ROBERT LOUIS STEVENSON

Make a list of the places you would most like to explore
simply by walking around them.

—7—

TRIP DIARY

WHERE

DATE

....

STANDOUT EXPERIENCE

....

....

....

THE MOMENT I'LL ALWAYS REMEMBER

....

....

....

SOMETHING NEW I LEARNED

....

PEOPLE I MET

....

FOOD I ATE

....

MUSIC I LISTENED TO

....

....

TOP 10
DESTINATIONS ON A BUDGET

Here are the best places to travel when you want to keep costs down.

1. Kyrgyzstan
Budget: $20 per day

There are no permit fees needed for hiking in (most of) Kyrgyzstan's mountain ranges, and the scenery is stunning.

2. Laos
Budget: $25 per day

Discover Kuang Si, one of the most beautiful waterfalls in the world, with an entry price of just $2.25.

3. Nepal
Budget: $25 per day

Stay in dorm accommodations for as little as $3 a night. In some regions if you pay to eat where you stay, your bed is free.

▶ 4. Bolivia
Budget: $25 per day

South America's most budget-friendly country is full of culture and sights.

5. Nicaragua
Budget: $35 per day

Enjoy the great outdoors with fabulous opportunities for surfing, volcano hiking, and diving.

6. Thailand
Budget: $35 per day

The further north you stay in Thailand, the further your money will stretch. Be aware that islands cost more than staying on the mainland.

7. Vietnam
Budget: $40 per day

Indulge in healthy and cheap street food. A bowl of pho or rice will cost you less than $2.

8. Turkey
Budget: $50 per day

Bathe in the ancient Pamukkale thermal pools for just $5.50.

9. Portugal
Budget: $50 per day

Book a surf camp where your equipment, lessons, and accommodation are all included.

10. Bulgaria
Budget: $55 per day

Soak up great European architecture and culture at a fraction of the price of its western neighbors.

8

TRIP DIARY

WHERE   DATE

....

STANDOUT EXPERIENCE

....

....

....

THE MOMENT I'LL ALWAYS REMEMBER

....

....

....

SOMETHING NEW I LEARNED

....

PEOPLE I MET

....

FOOD I ATE

....

MUSIC I LISTENED TO

....

....

A NOMAD I WILL REMAIN FOR LIFE, IN LOVE WITH DISTANT AND UNCHARTED PLACES.

ISABELLE EBERHARDT

Where would you most like to visit all by yourself?

—9—

TRIP DIARY

WHERE

DATE

....

STANDOUT EXPERIENCE

....

....

THE MOMENT I'LL ALWAYS REMEMBER

....

....

SOMETHING NEW I LEARNED

....

PEOPLE I MET

....

FOOD I ATE

....

MUSIC I LISTENED TO

....

....

—10—

TRIP DIARY

WHERE   DATE

....

STANDOUT EXPERIENCE

....

....

....

THE MOMENT I'LL ALWAYS REMEMBER

....

....

....

SOMETHING NEW I LEARNED

....

PEOPLE I MET

....

FOOD I ATE

....

MUSIC I LISTENED TO

....

....

TOP 20
WILDLIFE VACATIONS

Incredible animal adventures—experience the best of nature.

▶ 1. Kruger National Park for Africa's Big Five
South Africa

Be awed by elephants, rhinos, lions, leopards, buffalo, and so much more.

2. Florida Springs for manatees
Florida

Call it a sea cow, call it a dugong, there's nothing quite like a manatee.

3. Johnstone Strait for orcas
Vancouver Island, Canada

Kayak into the bay to marvel at the antics of pods of orcas.

4. Bwindi Impenetrable Forest National Park for gorillas
Uganda

Lose all sense of time as you watch gorillas at rest.

5. Colca Canyon for condors
Peru

Watch condors soar where they have flown for thousands of years.

6. Ranthambore National Park for tigers
Rajasthan, India

Be one of the lucky ones who manages to see a wild tiger on the prowl.

7. Kangaroo Island for kangaroos and koalas
Australia

Fall in love with Australia's famous marsupials.

8. Tortuguero National Park for toucans
Costa Rica

Who can spot a toucan—one of the world's most impressively billed birds?

9. Demilitarized Zone for cranes
South Korea

Be struck by the elegance of the white-naped crane.

10. Jigokudani Park for snow monkeys
Japan

Is there anything more sensible than a cold monkey in a hot bath?

11. Mindo for birds
Ecuador

The color and number of birds in the cloud forest has to be seen to be believed.

12. Galápagos Islands for wonders
Ecuador

Wildlife like nowhere else on Earth—literally.

13. Punta Tombo for penguins
Patagonia, Argentina

Wander among the world's best waddlers.

14. Snow safari
Lapland, Finland

Lynx, mountain hares, arctic foxes, snow grouse, wolves, wolverines—see them all from a pair of cross-country skis.

15. Yellowstone National Park
Wyoming

Come for the bears, stay for the moose . . . and the wolves, bison, otters, and elks.

16. Chengdu Research Base of Giant Panda Breeding
Chengdu, China
Few things are as iconic as a bamboo-munching panda bear.

17. Pantanal
Brazil
Pink river dolphins, anacondas, piranhas, monkeys—this wetland area is a wildlife enthusiast's dream.

18. Ranomafana National Park
Madagascar
Visit the Galápagos of Africa to see all types of lemurs.

19. Westman Islands for puffins
Iceland
Admire the puffin's perfect plumage.

20. Danum Valley for orangutans
Borneo
Witness one of our most endangered species.

—11—

TRIP DIARY

WHERE

DATE

....

STANDOUT EXPERIENCE

....

....

THE MOMENT I'LL ALWAYS REMEMBER

....

....

SOMETHING NEW I LEARNED

....

PEOPLE I MET

....

FOOD I ATE

....

MUSIC I LISTENED TO

....

....

PEOPLE ARE CAPABLE, AT ANY TIME IN THEIR LIVES, OF DOING WHAT THEY DREAM OF.

PAULO COELHO

What do you dream of doing, and what do you need to make those dreams a reality?

....
....
....
....
....
....
....
....
....

—12—

TRIP DIARY

WHERE

DATE

....

STANDOUT EXPERIENCE

....

....

....

THE MOMENT I'LL ALWAYS REMEMBER

....

....

....

SOMETHING NEW I LEARNED

....

PEOPLE I MET

....

FOOD I ATE

....

MUSIC I LISTENED TO

....

....

TOP 20
PLACES TO SWIM OR DIVE

Whether you are a skinny dipper or an avid diver, always check with the locals before you jump in.

▶ 1. Ocean pools, Sydney
Various locations, Sydney, Australia
From Mona Vale to Bondi Beach, these amazing pools allow you to swim in the ocean—no sharks allowed!

2. Seljavallalaug Swimming Pool
Seljavellir, Iceland
A lonely geothermal pool nestled in a lush green valley. What's not to love?

3. Dahab
Red Sea, Egypt
If you only ever snorkel in one place in your life, make it here. It will blow your mind how much activity there is below the surface.

4. Cenotes LabnaHa
Tulum, Mexico
Jump into the stunning blue water of this sinkhole surrounded by verdant, rocky ledges.

5. Great Blue Hole
Lighthouse Reef, Belize
This perfectly circular, giant marine sinkhole looks amazing and is home to the beautifully named butterfly fish, midnight parrotfish, and angelfish.

6. Coral Gardens
Sipadan, Malaysia
There's a reason Jacques Cousteau described this spot as "an untouched piece of art." It's stunning.

7. Giola Lagoon
Thassos Beaches, Greece
Jump from the rocks into this secret seaside lagoon.

8. Finolhu
Maldives
Look no further for those perfect turquoise seas and white, white sands.

9. Heron Island
Great Barrier Reef, Australia
With twenty different dive sites, this is the place to see big marine life and intricate, colorful coral.

10. Darwin's Arch
Galápagos Islands, Ecuador
Above the sea, a stunning rock formation; below, schools of whale sharks, hammerheads, and seals.

11. Havasu Falls
Grand Canyon, Arizona
Swim at the foot of this 100 ft (30 m) high waterfall—the 11 mi (18 km) hike is worth a reward.

12. Leven Bank
Unguja Island, Zanzibar, Tanzania
Some of the clearest waters you'll ever see and a stunning underwater landscape.

13. Blue Hole
Gozo, Malta
As impressive for its incredible rock formations as it is for its varied underwater life.

14. Likoma Island
Malawi
Great wide beaches, but fresh Lake Malawi water for swimming. A perfect combination.

15. Third Encounter
Saba, Dutch Caribbean

Marvel at the giant sponges on this otherworldly horseshoe-shaped seamount.

16. Anse Source d'Argent
La Digue, Seychelles

Curving palm trees, check. White sand, check. Turquoise waters, check. Giant boulders, check. Swim here? Please.

17. Playa Flamenco
Culebra, Puerto Rico

A little horseshoe-shaped slice of Caribbean perfection.

18. Richelieu Rock
Mu Ko Surin National Park, Thailand

Renowned for its spectacular marine life with abundant tuna, barracuda, and sharks.

19. Cocos Islands
Costa Rica

Honestly, the thirty-six-hour boat ride is worth it to dive among schools of surreal hammerheads.

20. Cleetwood Cove
Crater Lake, Oregon

You can swim in not just a lake in the crater of an extinct volcano, but in stunning mountains to boot.

—13—

TRIP DIARY

WHERE   DATE

....

STANDOUT EXPERIENCE

....

....

....

THE MOMENT I'LL ALWAYS REMEMBER

....

....

....

SOMETHING NEW I LEARNED

....

PEOPLE I MET

....

FOOD I ATE

....

MUSIC I LISTENED TO

....

....

A TRAVELER WITHOUT OBSERVATION IS A BIRD WITHOUT WINGS.

MOSLIH EDDIN SAADI

What have you learned about the places you have been to?

....

....

....

....

....

....

....

....

....

....

—14—

TRIP DIARY

WHERE   DATE

....

STANDOUT EXPERIENCE

....

....

THE MOMENT I'LL ALWAYS REMEMBER

....

....

....

SOMETHING NEW I LEARNED

....

PEOPLE I MET

....

FOOD I ATE

....

MUSIC I LISTENED TO

....

....

IT IS BETTER TO SEE SOMETHING ONCE, THAN TO HEAR ABOUT IT A THOUSAND TIMES.

ASIAN PROVERB

Which unexpected moments or grand events are going to stay with you the longest?

—15—

TRIP DIARY

WHERE

DATE

....

STANDOUT EXPERIENCE

....

....

....

THE MOMENT I'LL ALWAYS REMEMBER

....

....

....

SOMETHING NEW I LEARNED

....

PEOPLE I MET

....

FOOD I ATE

....

MUSIC I LISTENED TO

....

....

TOP 20
TRAILS FOR HIKING

If you plan to hike, always prepare well and check with local experts before you set off.

1. Torres del Paine National Park
Southern Chile

With soaring pinnacles, glaciers, turquoise lakes, and great paths, Chile's national park in the wilderness is hard to beat.

▶ 2. Trolltunga
Skjeggedal, Norway

A tough hike for an awe-inspiring view from the "troll's tongue" over Ringedalsvatnet lake.

3. West Coast Trail
Pacific Rim National Park Reserve, Vancouver Island, Canada

With ladders, mud, and waist-deep water, this is a tough but sensational backcountry hike.

4. Everest Base Camp
Himalayas, Nepal

Iconic by name, stunning by nature.

5. Cinque Terre
La Spezia, Italy

Five colorful seaside villages, one meandering trail through olive trees and vineyards. Pure joy.

6. Lycian Way
Fethiye to Anatalya, Turkey

Mediterranean views, crumbling ruins, secluded beaches—you'll find it all on the 335 mi (540 km) long-distance path.

7. Inca Trail
Cuzco, Peru

Four days of hiking on ancient paths to be met with the splendors of Machu Picchu when you finish.

8. Hoàng Liên Son Mountains
Sa Pa, Vietnam

Fill your lungs with the glorious air of these lush mountains with their terraced rice fields.

9. West Highland Way
Glasgow to Fort William, Scotland

Immerse yourself in Scotland's rugged and beautiful highlands.

10. Appalachian Trail
Eastern United States

The world's longest hiking trail crosses fantastic scenery in fourteen states.

11. Bashō Wayfarer
Tohoku region, Japan

Be inspired by the poet Matsuo Bashō on this six-day trek with fabulous views.

12. GR20
Corsica, France

Known as one of the world's most challenging treks, it is also one of the most varied and beautiful.

13. Kalalau Trail
Kauai, Hawaii

This 11 mi (18 km) beach-to-beach trail is full of drama as it crosses five lush valleys and creeps along towering sea cliffs.

14. La Ciudad Perdida
Santa Marta, Colombia

Trek through dense rain forest to a lost Tayrona city hidden in the hills.

15. Great Ocean Walk
Victoria, Australia
Drink in the views from this stunning 62 mi (100 km) trail.

16. Tour du Mont Blanc
France and Italy
Feel alive in the hills on this circumnavigation of Mont Blanc at the heart of the Alps.

17. Mount Kilimanjaro
Tanzania
Climb to the top of Africa with an ascent of Mount Kilimanjaro.

18. Tongariro Alpine Crossing
North Island, New Zealand
Experience dramatic scenery, bright turquoise lakes, and picture-perfect volcanoes on this epic trek.

19. Camino de Santiago
Northern Spain
Of all the routes on offer for this epic pilgrimage, choose the one through the beautiful hills of northern Spain.

20. Pennine Way
Northern England, United Kingdom
Stride up the backbone of England through stunning and varied countryside.

—16—

TRIP DIARY

WHERE   DATE

....

STANDOUT EXPERIENCE

....

....

....

THE MOMENT I'LL ALWAYS REMEMBER

....

....

....

SOMETHING NEW I LEARNED

....

PEOPLE I MET

....

FOOD I ATE

....

MUSIC I LISTENED TO

....

....

WE WANDER FOR DISTRACTION, BUT WE TRAVEL FOR FULFILLMENT.

HILAIRE BELLOC

How do you think your adventures will change you for the future?

....

....

....

....

....

....

....

....

TRIP DIARY

WHERE

DATE

....

STANDOUT EXPERIENCE

....

....

....

THE MOMENT I'LL ALWAYS REMEMBER

....

....

....

SOMETHING NEW I LEARNED

....

PEOPLE I MET

....

FOOD I ATE

....

MUSIC I LISTENED TO

....

....

TOP 20
CULTURAL FESTIVALS

Whether you are looking for an uplifting experience or one of the greatest large-scale parties on Earth, here are twenty of the world's best celebrations.

▶ 1. Holi Festival
Goa, India

Join this Hindu springtime festival, when strangers drench each other in color.

2. Day of the Dead
Mexico City, Mexico

Don your best face paint and celebrate the lives of your ancestors.

3. Carnival
Rio de Janeiro, Brazil

Dance until dawn at the greatest street party of them all.

4. Burning Man
Black Rock Desert, Nevada

Create a city full of art where anything can happen.

5. Songkran Water Festival
Chiang Mai, Thailand

Ring in the traditional Thai New Year with a proper soaking.

6. Oktoberfest
Munich, Germany

Drink in the biggest beer halls you'll ever see.

7. Diwali
Jaipur, India

Enjoy the world's best festival of light.

8. Harbin Ice and Snow Festival
Harbin, China

Wrap up warm and marvel at magnificent ice sculptures.

9. Mardi Gras
New Orleans, Louisiana

Put on your purple—or green or gold—and join the Mardi Gras parade.

10. Venice Carnival
Venice, Italy

Party incognito at this elaborate masked ball.

11. La Tomatina
Buñol, Spain

Throw a tomato at the world's biggest food fight.

12. Boryeong Mud Festival
Boryeong, South Korea

Frolic in the mud to your heart's content.

13. Hanami
Kyoto, Japan

Contemplate the world from under the cherry blossom.

14. Gerewol
Chad

Enjoy the beauty pageant of the Wodaabe men in their intricate and elaborate makeup.

15. Fiesta de la Candelaria
Puno, Peru

See the streets fill with color as 50,000 dancers come out to play.

16. Tet
Hanoi, Vietnam

Join the Vietnamese New Year celebrations as the city explodes into color.

17. Pushkar Camel Fair
Pushkar, Rajasthan, India
Celebrate the camel in all its colorful finery.

18. Fireball Festival
Nejapa, El Salvador
Imagine a snowball fight with fireballs; it's not for the fainthearted.

19. Shinnyo Lantern Floating
Honolulu, Hawaii
A peaceful—and beautiful—way to give thanks and remembrance.

20. New Year's Eve
Sydney, Australia
Be among the first to celebrate the New Year with one of the world's most epic firework displays.

—18—

TRIP DIARY

WHERE

DATE

....

STANDOUT EXPERIENCE

....

....

....

THE MOMENT I'LL ALWAYS REMEMBER

....

....

....

SOMETHING NEW I LEARNED

....

PEOPLE I MET

....

FOOD I ATE

....

MUSIC I LISTENED TO

....

....

TOP 20
PUBLIC WORKS OF ART

There is no need to visit a museum to see amazing art.
Here are twenty inspiring works you can see for free.

1. Rothko Chapel
Houston, Texas

Spend time in quiet contemplation surrounded by fourteen Rothko works of art.

2. Sea Organ
Zadar, Croatia

Experience the sounds of the sea, as waves create music through an organ.

3. *Puppy*
Bilbao, Spain

Embrace the kitsch with Jeff Koons's 40 ft (12 m) flower-powered *Puppy*.

4. *Angel of the North*
Gateshead, England

Walk beneath the wings of Antony Gormley's rusted steel angel.

▼ 5. Banksy in Bethlehem
Bethlehem, Palestine

Feel the power of Banksy's artworks along the separation wall in the West Bank.

6. *Le Nomade*
Antibes, France

Gaze out to sea in the company of this traveler by Jaume Plensa.

7. Godzilla head
Shinjuku, Tokyo, Japan

Few sculptures seem quite as apt as Godzilla staring over a movie theater in Tokyo.

8. *Spiral Jetty*
Rozel Point, Utah

Follow the contours of Robert Smithson's *Spiral Jetty* on the Great Salt Lake.

9. Nelson Mandela (*Release* sculpture)
Howick, South Africa

Retrace the great man's long walk to freedom and watch as fifty steel columns form into his portrait.

10. *Ali and Nino*
Batumi, Georgia

Each night Tamara Kvesitadze's two 26 ft (8 m) tall steel lovers pass through each other, embrace for a moment then part forever.

11. *Refuge d'Art*
Hautes-Alpes, France

Stumble upon fabulous Andy Goldsworthy creations on this hiking route in the Alps.

12. *Federation Bells*
Melbourne, Australia

Musicians can submit their own compositions to be played on this installation of bells—truly public art.

13. *Les Voyageurs*
Marseilles, France
See travel differently through Bruno Catalano's travelers with large sections of their bodies missing.

14. *Shoes on the Danube Bank*
Budapest, Hungary
Feel moved at this memorial to Hungarian Jews.

15. *People of the River*
Singapore
Trace the history of the city through the bronze people created by Chong Fah Cheong.

16. **Gibbs Farm**
Makarau, New Zealand
Possibly the world's best collection of outdoor art. It's free, but you have to book in advance to see it.

▲ 17. *Cloud Gate*
Chicago, Illinois
Anish Kapoor's shiny metal bean makes you marvel at how metal can seem so toylike.

18. *Tree Mountain*
Ylöjärvi, Finland
Planted in a spiral on a man-made mountain, these firs are art that grows and grows.

19. **Sculptures by children**
Princess Ingrid Alexandra Sculpture Park, Palace Park, Oslo, Norway
Feel young at heart in this sculpture park where the art is created by children.

20. *Digital Orca*
Vancouver, Canada
Ponder on the nature of Vancouver next to Douglas Coupland's pixelated killer whale.

—19—

TRIP DIARY

WHERE   DATE

....

STANDOUT EXPERIENCE

....

....

THE MOMENT I'LL ALWAYS REMEMBER

....

....

SOMETHING NEW I LEARNED

....

PEOPLE I MET

....

FOOD I ATE

....

MUSIC I LISTENED TO

....

....

SURELY, OF ALL THE WONDERS OF THE WORLD, THE HORIZON IS THE GREATEST.

FREYA STARK

What mountains, hills, and towers do you want to climb to reach new horizons?

—20—
TRIP DIARY

WHERE

DATE

....

STANDOUT EXPERIENCE

....

....

....

THE MOMENT I'LL ALWAYS REMEMBER

....

....

....

SOMETHING NEW I LEARNED

....

PEOPLE I MET

....

FOOD I ATE

....

MUSIC I LISTENED TO

....

....

NOT ALL THOSE WHO WANDER ARE LOST.

J.R.R. TOLKIEN

TOP TIPS
HOW TO PLAN
A TRIP

1

Decide where to go
Think about what you want to get from a trip and which place will offer you the best opportunities.

2

Buy a good guidebook
The internet has lots of great sites and blogs, but a dedicated book will generally have been more stringently checked.

3

Research when the best time to travel is
Based on weather, national holidays, rainy seasons, off-season flight deals, etc.

4

Calculate how long you want to go for
This could be influenced by your budget, a job offer, or even an unmissable family occasion.

5

Work out how much your trip will cost
As well as a per-day living budget, include the cost of flights, travel insurance, etc.

6

Start saving
Set yourself a weekly target; this can help break down what seems like a huge amount into workable goals.

7

Plan with your friends
Persuade your friends to start saving too, if you're planning on traveling with people.

8

Look for deals
Keep an eye out for good flight deals or those that can be bought with points, and look into the option of a stopover.

9

Book flights
Always do this through a reputable company and ensure you are covered for any unforeseen events.

10

Enjoy your trip!
Go with an open mind, stick to your budget, keep in touch with home, and you'll have a wonderful experience.

BEFORE YOU GO

Before you embark on a trip, there is a fair bit of admin that needs to be taken care of. Use the checklist below to make sure you have everything in order.

PASSPORT

Check that this document is valid for at least six months beyond your travel dates. Make a note of your passport details on page 190 just in case it gets lost or stolen.

✓

Passport expires on

VISAS

Make a note of different visa requirements for the countries you are visiting.

Country   *Visa requirements*

VACCINATIONS

Some countries require proof of your vaccination history before they will let you in.

Country   *Vaccine needed*

ADVANCE BOOKINGS

Some of your bucket list ideas will require advance bookings (for example, the Inca Trail), even before you choose a flight date.

Event   *Booking agreed for what date*

CHECKLIST
PACKING ESSENTIALS

List electrics and chargers/adapters, toiletries, clothing, and other
essentials like a flashlight, contact lenses, or medications.

UNDERSTANDING
POWER OUTLETS

Check which adapter you need before you travel. Ensure that your tech can cope with any change in voltage too, which can vary from place to place. Here are the plug/socket shapes you may encounter.

TYPE A
USA, Canada, Mexico, and Japan

TYPE B
USA, Canada, Mexico, and Japan

TYPE C
Europe (excluding UK and Ireland), South America, and Asia

TYPE D
India

TYPE E
France, Belgium, Poland, Slovakia, and Czechia

TYPE F
Europe (excluding the UK and Ireland) and Russia

TYPE G
UK, Ireland, Malta, Malaysia, and Singapore

TYPE H
Israel

TYPE I
Australia, New Zealand, China, and Argentina

TYPE J
Switzerland and Liechtenstein

TYPE K
Denmark and Greenland

TYPE L
Italy and Chile

TYPE M
South Africa

TYPE N
Brazil and South Africa

TYPE O
Thailand

USEFUL PHRASES
TO MASTER

Learning a few simple words and phrases in a foreign language is well worth the time when you're traveling. Start a conversation with people you meet, show interest in local culture, and, most importantly, make yourself understood.

Before you depart—while you still have easy access to the internet, perhaps—you can jot down these useful phrases to rely on during your travels. Alternatively, you can ask someone you meet along the way to help you say the following useful sayings and expressions.

PHRASES TO LOOK UP BEFORE YOU GO

✓

○ Hello ....

○ Good morning ....

○ Good-bye ....

○ Please ....

○ Thank you ....

○ Excuse me ....

○ Sorry ....

○ How are you? ....

I only speak a little . . .

I don't understand

Yes / No

Where is the bathroom?

Exit / Entrance

Numbers 1–10

I would like . . . /Can I have . . . ?

That is good/bad

Do you sell . . . ?

Where is the station?

How much does it cost?

I don't eat . . .

Can I get the bill please?

Where can I wash my hands?

Can I pay by card?

Do you have a spare . . . ?

EMERGENCY
BACKUP

If the worst happens and difficult situations do arise while you're on your travels, they can be made much less stressful if you have all the contacts you need close at hand.

Fill in this page before you depart and leave a copy of it with somebody back home so that they have all your crucial information too.

WHO ELSE CAN YOUR FAMILY CALL IF THEY CANNOT GET THROUGH TO YOU IN AN EMERGENCY

Name .... *Number* ....

Name .... *Number* ....

YOUR PASSPORT

Number .... *Expiration date* ....

YOUR TRAVEL INSURANCE

Provided by .... *Policy number* ....

Telephone number for medical emergencies .... *Telephone number for all other claims* ....

WHO YOU NEED TO CALL FOR LOST OR STOLEN CARDS

Bank .... *Telephone number* ....

Card number ....

EMERGENCY NUMBERS IN COUNTRIES YOU'RE VISITING

Country | *Number*

EMBASSY CONTACT DETAILS IN COUNTRIES YOU'RE VISITING

Country | *Address* | *Number*

YOUR FLIGHT DETAILS

Date | *Flight no.* | *From* | *Departure time* | *To* | *Arrival time*

IMAGE CREDITS